CARD GAMES

GAMES

for Children

Crocodile

CARD GAMES

for Children

by Len Collis

Illustrated by
Terry Carter and Bob George

Published in Great Britain 1989
by Crocodile Books Ltd
1 - 6 Grand Parade, Brighton BN2 2QB, East Sussex.

© David Booth (Publishing) Ltd 1983

ISBN 1-85136-020-4

Printed in Italy

Introduction

Good card games have a habit of turning up all over the world and we have tried to put them all in this book.

But that's a problem, because every country seems to choose a different name (sometimes several names!) and quite often the rules are slightly different, too.

For this book we've chosen the versions we think are the most fun, and put them down under the names by which they're best known.

For instance, the hilarious game of *Old Maid* is called by that name in most English-speaking countries, and that's the title it's given here.

But we've also included another version (which some people think is better) that's very popular in France. Children there call it *Le Pouilleux,* so that's what we've called it, too.

You've probably realized by now that there are hundreds and hundreds of different games you can play with a single deck of cards.

But do you know anything about the cards themselves? Not many people do. So before you start playing, learn some of their secrets...

Have you ever looked closely at a pack of playing cards? If you have, you've probably noticed how strange it really is.

First, there are the crazy clothes worn by the court cards, the kings, queens, and jacks. The last time anyone dressed like that in real life was nearly 500 years ago!

Then there's the fancy design on the ace of spades. The other aces are plain, so why does the ace of spades have to be different?

And what about the joker? How did he get into the pack?

Playing cards are so old that nobody knows who invented them or where they came from. The packs we play with today aren't very different from those of centuries ago, which is why the characters on court cards are still in their medieval clothes.

The two cards that are different are the joker and the ace of spades.

The joker didn't exist at all until a game called Euchre became popular in America during the 1870s. To play it, you needed a pack with an extra card. When the game caught on in Europe, card makers added a blank card, the *"Euchre card"*, to each pack. But somehow the name was misheard or more likely misspelled and *"Euchre"* became *"Joker"*.

4

The card turned out to be very popular and we've been stuck with the joker ever since.

There's also an amazing story behind the drawing of the ace of spades. At one time in Britain, playing cards were heavily taxed! This made them very expensive to buy. As you can imagine, it was a very unpopular tax and plenty of people found ways not to pay it.

To outwit the tax-dodgers, the British government passed an incredible law. They made it *illegal* for card makers to print any aces of spades!

All card companies had to buy their aces of spades from the government's own printers, and pay the tax at the same time. To make it difficult for forgers, an engraved crown-and-scroll design with the card maker's name underneath was printed on each ace.

It's hard to believe such an odd idea could ever work. But it did and the law, which came in during the eighteenth century, lasted nearly one hundred years.

When it was finally scrapped, so many people around the world had become used to seeing a fancy drawing on the ace of spades that the card makers kept the idea going.

Learn what these words mean first...

Cut You do this by lifting some of the cards from the top of the pack. Sometimes, players *"cut"* in turn to see which cards they expose. The player who shows the highest card then deals first.

It's also usual for the player on the dealer's left to *"cut"* the pack (returning the top bundle of cards to the bottom of the deck) after it has been shuffled so that the dealer can't be accused of cheating.

Deal means distributing cards to each of the players taking part. They normally get a card in turn.

Deck means the standard set of 52 playing cards.

Face down means you can only see the backs of the cards laid on the table.

Face up means the opposite of face down.

Hand means the cards you are holding.

6

Pack is another word for deck.

Pair means any two cards of the same value like two jacks or two aces.

Picture card is a king, queen, or jack.

Shuffle means mixing up the cards so that they are in a different (and unknown) order. It's usual to give cards a good shuffle before starting a game.

Spot card is any card in the pack except a king, queen, or jack.

Suit means a set of cards of the same design. There are four suits in every pack—hearts, diamonds, spades, and clubs.

Trick means the cards placed face up on the table, one by each player, in a single round of play.

Trump is a superstar card! It comes from a suit that has been chosen by the players to have special powers. Normally, cards of the trump suit beat all others.

Wastepile is a stack of cards that have been used up during play.

Wild cards are cards that count as anything you want. You can usually play a wild card in place of any other.

Contents

Good games for one

Good games for two

Good games for three or more

Good games for the family

Good games for one

Beehive

Number of Players: 1

Number of Cards: 52

This is a super game to play when you are left by yourself with nothing to do.

Start by dealing a stack of 10 cards face down on the table. Then turn the whole pile over so that the bottom card is face up on top. This is your beehive.

Now deal 6 cards in a row, all face up. This is the garden.

Start by looking for any pairs showing

START BY LOOKING FOR PAIRS.

(2 fours, 2 queens, any 2 cards of the same value). If you find a pair, place one card on top of the other and fill the space with a card from the top of the beehive.

The idea is to build up your garden piles so that they contain all 4 cards of the same value (4 aces, maybe, or 4 tens). When this happens, put the 4 to one side and start a new pile with the top card from the beehive.

Sometimes the card on the beehive itself makes one of a pair. Good! Put it out in the garden–never add on to the beehive.

When you've started as many garden piles as you can, and filled the empty spaces with cards from the beehive, you're ready for the real action!

Take the undealt part of the pack (this is called the *"stock"*) and hold it face down. Now count off a batch of 3 cards. Place this batch face up on the table to start a wastepile.

Now look to see if the card showing on top of the wastepile can be added to any of the piles in the garden.

If it can be paired off, fine. Go ahead and put it in place. This leaves the next card of the wastepile showing. Perhaps that can be matched, too? If not, count another 3 from the stock and add a second batch to the wastepile.

And so on until all the stock has been

STOCK

WASTEPILE

COUNT OFF
BATCHES OF THREE
CARDS AT A TIME.

transferred, 3 cards at a time, onto the wastepile.

Be careful not to change the order of the cards, and make sure the card you play from the wastepile is always the top one (it's cheating to play any other!).

When there are no more cards left in your hand, pick up the wastepile without shuffling it, turn it over to form a new stock, and go through it again.

You can do this as many times as you like until you win the game or are blocked. After all the cards in the beehive have been used up, you may fill spaces in the garden with top cards from the wastepile.

You win when the entire pack has been sorted into 4s of the same value and there are no more piles left in the garden.

Sir Tommy is a real *"golden oldie"* and has been causing Patience players to lose their patience for years.

The game itself is maddeningly simple, but it's a toughie to win. So be prepared to start tearing your hair out!

Start by giving the cards a good shuffle. Then hold the pack face down and deal the top card. Turn it face up on the table, praying that it's an ace. (The chances are 12 to 1 against).

No ace? Too bad. Try again with the next card. And the next and the next and the next. Eventually one must come up!

Meanwhile, make 4 heaps, face up, out of the no-good cards. If you want, you can have lots of cards in one heap and just a few in the others.

Later on, those heaps, and the order of the cards in them, are going to be important, which is why you're allowed to add on to any heap you choose.

At last, an ace! Now you can get going.

14

Place it face up on the table away from the heaps and look around for a two to put on it.

The two must must be the top card on one of the heaps but it doesn't need to be of the same suit as the ace. If you have been able to find a two, look for a three. Again it can be any suit. Continue until you've built up a complete stack on top of the ace in correct sequence from the two to the king.

If none of the 4 top cards on the heaps is the one you want, continue dealing. Start a fresh stack with every ace that turns up, and get sequences going on all of them. The idea is to clear all the heaps and finish with 4 complete stacks, each running from ace to king.

It can be done, but you must be clever to avoid trapping desperately needed cards at the bottom of the 4 heaps.

Just try not to let the whole business drive you crazy!

*MAKE FOUR PILES AS YOU HUNT FOR **ACES**...*

Clock Patience

Number of Players: **1**

Number of Cards: **52**

Shuffle the pack and then deal 13 piles of 4 cards each, all face down. Now arrange 12 of the piles in a circle, putting them in the same places as the numbers on a clock dial. The thirteenth pile goes in the middle of the circle.

Start by turning up the top card of the

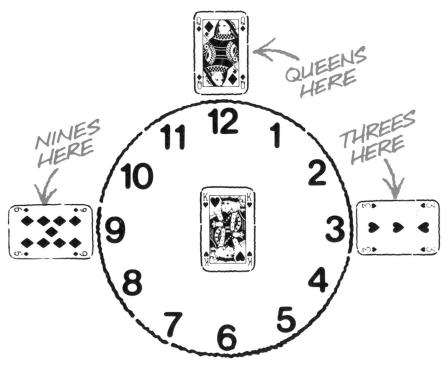

middle pile. Suppose it's a seven. Slide it face up under the 4 cards in the 7 o'clock position, and pick up the top card of the pile. Let's say it's a queen. Shove that under the 12 o'clock pile, and take one from the top of the same pile. It might be a three. Put that under the 3 o'clock heap, and take off the top card. And so on.

Jacks go on the 11 o'clock space, queens in 12 o'clock, kings in the middle. The idea is to finish with all the cards face up in their proper places.

But beware: it won't work out if all 4 kings turn up before the rest are safely home!

Eleven Up

Number of Players: 1

Number of Cards: 52

Fed up with patience games you never win? If you are, cheer yourself up with Eleven Up.

Shuffle the pack and deal out a row of 9 cards all face up.

Cover any picture cards (jacks, queens, and kings) that you see. You do this by placing another card face up over the picture card.

Then cover any 2 spot cards that add up to

A GOOD START!

NOW COVER-UP PICTURE CARDS AND PAIRS THAT ADD UP TO 11!

11 (a seven and four maybe, or a nine and two).

Continue covering up as many cards as you can. Remember, they must be pairs of spot cards that add up to 11, or picture cards.

The idea is to deal out all the cards in your hand. It works about twice in every 3 games.

This is similar to Eleven Up, but harder to win! First, deal out 9 cards all face up.

Remove any 2 spot cards that add up to 11 (like a five and six), and deal out more cards to fill the empty spaces.

COLLECT PAIRS THAT ADD UP TO 11, BUT LEAVE PICTURE CARDS UNTIL JACK, QUEEN, KING ARE SHOWING.

Leave any picture cards where they are until a jack, queen and king are all showing, then remove all 3.

Continue taking out as many cards as you can, plugging each gap with cards from your hand.

To win you must finish up holding no cards, and there mustn't be any left on the table either.

It's a toughie, but you should manage to clear the lot about once every 7 attempts.

This is a bit like Eleven Up and Eleven Away. First, take out the 4 tens and put them on one side. They're not needed.

Shuffle the other 48 cards, and deal 16 face up in 4 rows of 4.

Remove any cards of the same suit that add up to 15 (for example, the seven and eight of clubs) and deal more cards to fill the empty spaces.

Aces count as ones in this game. So you could make up 15 from say, a seven, four, three,

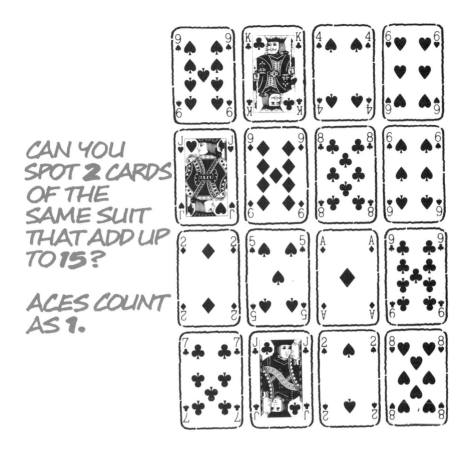

CAN YOU
SPOT **2** CARDS
OF THE
SAME SUIT
THAT ADD UP
TO **15**?

ACES COUNT
AS **1.**

and ace (but they must be from the same suit).

Leave any picture cards where they are until a jack, queen, and king of the same suit are all showing, then remove the 3 together.

Continue taking away as many cards as you can, and filling gaps with fresh ones.

The idea is to get rid of all the cards in your hand, and clear the table as well.

It can be done, and more often than you think.

You need only the high cards in the pack to play Wish, so before you start, take out all the twos, three, fours, fives, and sixes. That should leave just 32.

Start by giving those a good shuffle. Then hold them face down and count off a batch of 4 cards. Place this batch face up on the table. Deal another 4 and place them face up alongside the first batch.

DEAL 8 LOTS OF FOUR CARDS— THEN LOOK FOR PAIRS...

Continue to lay down batches of 4 until you have 8 separate piles on the table (and no more cards in your hand).

Now lift off the top cards in pairs, say, 2 jacks, 2 tens, or 2 aces, and put them on a wastepile.

22

Remove as many pairs as you can for as long as you can. But remember, you are only allowed to pair off top cards, not the ones underneath.

You win when all the cards are paired and the piles have been cleared away.

It works out more often than you think.

Here's a game that needs plenty of patience, because it's easy to play but hard to win.

First, give the cards a good shuffle. Then hold the pack face down in one hand, and peel off the top card. Place it face up on the table and call out, "Ace!"

Take the next card from the pack, place it face up on top of the previous one, and call, "Two!" Add a third card and call, "Three!" Then play a fourth and say, "Four!"

Continue like this, turning up a card at a time, and counting as you go. On the eleventh card, call, "Jack!"; on the twelfth say, "Queen!", and on the thirteenth, "King!" After that, begin

"MISS" CARDS

COUNT
AS YOU GO!

"HIT" CARDS

counting from "Ace" again.

Whenever the card you call is actually the same as the one you turn up, you've scored a hit! Throw each hit card to one side. When you've dealt the entire pack, pick up the pile from the table, turn it over, and start again. But make sure you continue counting from the place you left off.

The idea is to hit every card in the pack and finish empty-handed. But you're not allowed to shuffle the cards once you've started, and you lose if you go through the pack twice in succession without a single hit.

Patience

Number of Players: 1

Number of Cards: 52

Patience, also known as Solitaire, must be the most famous one-player card game in the world, and probably the most difficult to win. Start by giving the pack a good shuffle.

Then deal out a row of 7 cards. Make sure the first card in the row is face up, and the rest are face down.

Below these, deal a second row of 6 cards. They should overlap the face-down cards in the top row. As before, make sure that the first card in the row is face up, and the rest are face down.

Then deal a third row, this time of 5 cards. Once more, they overlap the face-down cards in the row above. And so on until you complete a triangle of 28 cards in 7 columns, looking like the layout in our picture.

Now study the 7 face-up cards. If any of them are aces, you're in luck! Remove them at once and place them to one side: you'll need them as base cards for collection piles. Turn over the next card in the column, above where each ace was, to keep 7 cards still showing.

No aces? Don't worry, there's still plenty of time to find some.

Look again at the face-up cards. This time, search for any cards in sequence. You need cards that follow each other in number, like a seven, eight, and nine, or a king, queen and jack.

If you find, say, a seven and eight, you can remove the seven from its column and overlap it on the eight, as long as the two cards are different colours.

PUT RED CARDS ON BLACK CARDS AND BLACK CARDS ON RED CARDS!

You can't put a red seven on a red eight, or a black queen on a black king. The cards must go red-on-black or black-on-red. And they must run in correct sequence, with the highest at the top and the lowest at the bottom.

But you can join sequences together if they crop up. For instance, you could add a seven, eight, nine sequence to a jack, ten sequence (provided that the red and black cards alternate correctly).

Each time you remove a card (or a sequence) from its column, turn over the card above and pray for an ace to show up. Eventually the 4 aces should appear (unless your luck is very bad!) and you can begin building your collections.

The idea is to make a complete stack on top of each ace in the correct suit and sequence from two to king.

So, once you've freed an ace, look for the correct two to put on it. The two must be of the same suit as the ace. And it must also be the last card in one of the sequences, or a face-up card at the foot of a column.

If you have been able to find two, look for three, and so on until your stack is complete. But remember, you can't take face-down cards or those trapped in sequences.

When you've started as many sequences and piles as you can, you're ready to tackle the next stage.

Take the undealt part of the pack and hold it face down. Then count off a batch of 3 cards. Place this batch face up on the table to start a wastepile.

Now look to see if the card on top of the wastepile can be added to a sequence or a collection.

STOCK

COUNT OFF BATCHES OF THREE CARDS AT A TIME.

WASTEPILE

If it can, put it in place. This will leave the next card of the wastepile showing. Perhaps that can be added somewhere, too. If not, count another 3 from the stock and add them to the wastepile. And so on until all the stock has been transferred, 3 cards at a time, onto the wastepile.

Be careful not to change the order of the cards, and make sure that the card you play from the wastepile is always the top one. (It's cheating to play any other!)

When there are no more cards left in your hand, pick up the wastepile without shuffling it, turn it over to form a new stock, and go through it again.

You can do this as many times as you like until you win the game or are blocked. When any of the columns run out of cards, you're allowed to fill the space, but only with a king, any other card is forbidden. If there's a king showing in another column, you can move it over, together with any sequence that's built on it. If not, you'll have to wait until a king shows up in the wastepile.

You win when the entire pack is collected into suits stacked in sequence on top of the 4 aces.

If you manage to make it "come out" completely, give yourself a pat on the back, it rarely happens.

2 Good games for two 2

Baby Snap

Number of Players: 2

Number of Cards: 52

This is the first card game that thousands, and probably millions, of children ever learn.

You can teach it to toddlers in about 30 seconds flat, and after 2 minutes or so they'll probably start beating you! So if you're stuck with minding your 4-year-old brother or sister one rainy afternoon, this is the game to play. Before you begin, divide the pack in 2 so that you get half each. The cards must be held face down so that you can't see what you have. The first player lays a card face up in the middle of the table. The other player puts a card on top, again face up. The first player places another card on top of that. And so on in turn.

Sooner or later, 2 cards of the same kind (perhaps 2 fours or 2 queens) are played together.

The first person to spot the pair and call out "Snap!" wins all the cards on the table, and adds them to the bottom of the stack in his other hand. The loser is the one who runs out of cards first.

Beat Your Neighbour Out of Doors

Number of Players: 2

Number of Cards: 52

Here's an old one! Some people call it Beggar My Neighbour or Strip Jack Naked.

Only two can play, and each person is given half the pack. The cards must be held face down so that you can't see what you have.

The first player lays a card face up in the middle of the table. The other player puts a card on top. The first player places one on top of that. And so on in turn.

Sooner or later, an ace or a picture card is thrown. Now the fun starts!

The other player must top it with another ace or a picture card.

If the card that's been thrown is an ace, your opponent has 4 chances to cover it. If the first card she puts on top is a spot card, she plays again. If another spot card turns up, she goes again. If the third and fourth cards are also spot cards, she's lost! You can now pick up all the cards on the table and add them to your stack.

But if one of her 4 cards is an ace or a picture card, the tables are turned! Now you have to cover it in the same way.

You can play up to 4 cards over an ace, 3 over a king, 2 over a queen, and just one over a jack. If you lose, your opponent collects all the cards on the table, and plays the first card to start the new pile going.

The loser is the one who runs out of cards first!

ACES AND
PICTURE CARDS
WIN THE PILE!

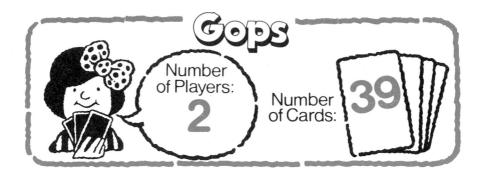

Gops

Number of Players: 2

Number of Cards: 39

Gops is an exciting game involving bluff and counter-bluff.

Before you start, remove the hearts from the pack. They are not required.

Then gather all the diamonds together, give them a good shuffle, and place them face down in a pile between you.

Finally, pass all the clubs to your opponent and keep all the spades for yourself.

To begin, turn over the top diamond and place it face up alongside the others.

Now choose a card from your own hand and lay it face down on the table in front of you. Wait for the other player to do the same.

When you're both ready, turn your 2 cards over. Whoever has laid the highest card (aces are low, kings are top) captures the diamond in the middle.

The king of diamonds counts 13 points, the queen 12, and the jack 10. The others are worth their spot numbers.

The winner takes the diamond, stores it face up on his side of the table, and turns up the next diamond in the pile. You play for this one exactly the same way as before. And so on until all the cards run out. Don't cover up any of the cards laid (or the diamonds played for) or you won't remember what's gone.

If you both play cards of the same value (say the seven of clubs against the seven of spades), it's a tie and the diamond remains in the middle. The winner of the next exchange then captures 2 diamonds, the one being played for and the card before. If you tie again, there are 3 cards to be won next time. And so on.

The winner is the player with the most points at the end. And the best bluffer!

PLAY TO WIN

EACH DIAMOND IN TURN.

Draw Hearts

Number of Players: **2**

Number of Cards: **52**

This is a 2-player version of Hearts (see page 64), and can be very exciting!

As in normal Hearts, you'll need to keep score, so find a pencil and paper before you begin. Shuffle the cards and deal out 13 to each player. Put the undealt part of the pack (called the "stock") face down on the table.

The first player (always the non-dealer) lays a card face up in the middle of the table.

The other player must now follow suit (which means he must play a card of the same suit as his opponent played).

If he has no card of that suit, he can put down any card, but it will count below the card his opponent led.

The person who plays the best card (aces are highest) wins the trick. He takes the top card off the stock to add to his hand (the loser takes the next card) and leads the first card of the following trick. And so on until all the stock is used up and the cards in hand are played out.

YOU COLLECT
FOUR PENALTY POINTS IF YOU WIN
THE KING OF HEARTS!

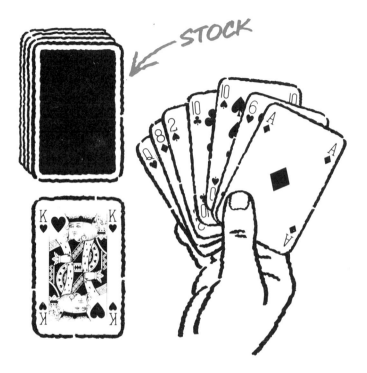

Like 4-player Hearts, the idea is to lose every trick containing a heart, especially the jack, queen, king, and the ace of hearts.

You pick up a penalty point for every spot card heart you win, 2 penalty points for the jack, 3 for the queen, 4 for the king, and 5 for the ace.

But if you manage to collect all 13 hearts, the penalty points are wiped out and you score zero!

The winner is the player with the lowest number of penalty points when the game ends.

Gin Rummy

Number of Players: **2**

Number of Cards: **52**

If you enjoy old movies on television, you'll almost certainly know something about Gin Rummy, even if you've never played it.

So many Hollywood films (funny ones, usually) have included a Gin Rummy scene that the game has become famous the world over!

Quite right, too, because Gin Rummy is one of the best games for 2 players ever invented. So it's well worth taking the trouble to learn.

HOLLYWOOD PRESENTS— GUNGA GIN!

To start, shuffle the cards and deal out 10 to each player. Put the undealt part of the pack face down on the table between you. Then turn over the top card and place it face up alongside the others to start a wastepile.

As in Rummy, the object of the game is to collect 3 or more cards that form a set (say, 3 queens or 4 twos) or a sequence (like the six, seven, eight, and nine of diamonds). Aces are low and count as one.

The idea is to get every card in your hand to form part of a sequence or set, and have nothing left over. If you manage this and can lay down all 10 cards at once (it's known as a *"gin"*), you win!

Your opponent (if you dealt) gets the first chance to improve his hand.

If he wants, he can swap one of the cards in his hand for the card lying face up by the stock.

MAKE **SETS** FROM THREE OR MORE CARDS OF THE SAME SORT...

MAKE **SEQUENCES** FROM THREE OR MORE CARDS OF THE SAME SUIT THAT RUN TOGETHER...

YOU LOSE POINTS FOR UNMATCHED CARDS...

If he doesn't want the card on the table, the chance passes to you.

If you don't want it either, it's your opponent's turn again. This time he must pick up the unknown top card from the stock.

He can keep the card he takes (if it's useful) and dump any other card in his hand on the wastepile. If the card from the stock is unwanted, it can go straight on the wastepile.

When he has made his choice, it's your turn again. You can choose either the top card on the wastepile or the unknown top card on the stock. After you've decided what to do, it's your opponent's turn again. And so on.

Then it's a race to see who can get the best hand first!

Remember, every unmatched card left in your hand when the game ends is given a penalty. You will collect 10 penalty points for each spare picture card, one penalty point for each ace, and the spot number on all the others.

As soon as you (or your opponent) collect a good enough hand, you can declare the game over.

You can do this at any time (when you've completed a turn) so long as the total number of unmatched cards left in your hand are worth 10 penalty points or less.

To stop the game, you call *"knock"* and

place your final card face down on the wastepile.

But beware! You must now lay all your cards, sets, sequences, and spare ones, face up on the table so that your opponent can see them.

And unless you have a gin, he can off-load unmatched cards of his own on to your sets and sequences. If for example, you lay down a set of 3 jacks, he can tag on the fourth jack if it's spare in his hand. Which could easily make his penalty points less than yours.

When both hands are laid on the table and the penalty points have been added up, you're ready to score. This is worked out in bonus marks.

For a gin, you score 25 bonus marks, plus one extra mark for every penalty point in your opponent's hand.

For a successful *"knock"*, you score the difference in penalty points between you.

For an unsuccessful *"knock"*, when your penalty points tally is the same as or more than your opponent's, your opponent gets 25 bonus marks plus the points difference (if any) between you. The first player to reach 100 bonus marks wins the game, and earns himself another 100 marks. On top of that, both players collect 25 marks for each hand they won along the way. If one of you fails to win a single hand, the other person scores a further 100 marks for the whitewash.

Round-the-Corner Gin

Number of Players: 2

Number of Cards: 52

If you enjoy Gin Rummy, you'll like this game, too. The basic play is the same as for Gin Rummy, so you must learn that game first. But there's an important difference.

In Round-the-Corner Gin, a sequence of cards can also go past the ace. This means you can lay a king, an ace, and a two of the same suit to make up a sequence, which can be a big help.

But be careful, any unmatched aces left in your hand at the end of play count 15 penalty points each.

Oklahoma Gin

Number of Players: **2**

Number of Cards: **52**

Many people play Oklahoma Gin thinking, in fact, that it's standard Gin Rummy. But they're wrong!

Oklahoma Gin has an extra rule, and it makes quite a lot of difference!

The basic play is the same as for Gin Rummy. But the card that's turned face up alongside the stock after the deal has a particular importance.

It fixes the number of penalty points you can have in your hand before you're allowed to *"knock."*

If, for instance, the face-up card is the seven of diamonds, you can't *"knock"* with more than

THE TURNED-UP CARD DECIDES THE NUMBER OF POINTS ALLOWED WHEN YOU "KNOCK"!

*WHEN AN ACE TURNS UP, YOU CAN'T **"KNOCK"** FOR LESS THAN **"GIN"**!*

7 penalty points in your hand.

If it's a four, you can't *"knock"* with more than 4 points. And so on.

Picture cards count as 10, and if an ace comes up you can't lay down your hand for less than a gin.

Spade Oklahoma

Number of Players: 2

Number of Cards: 52

You play this in the same way as Oklahoma Gin, but the scores for the hand are doubled if the face-up card after the deal happens to be a spade.

It can speed up or shatter your plans to win the game, so watch out!

3 Good games for three or more 3

Snap

Number of Players: 3 to 8

Number of Cards: 52

This is a good game for toddlers after they've mastered Baby Snap. The best number of people to play is probably 4 or 5, more than that and you risk a riot.

To begin, deal out all the cards one by one face down among the players. It doesn't matter if some get more than others.

Everybody must make a neat heap of their cards, keeping them face down.

TAKE OFF THE TOP CARD AND TURN IT OVER...

The first player (the person on the dealer's left) turns the top card of his heap face up, and places it on the table in front of him to start a pile. The next player does the same. So does the third player. And so on around the table.

THE FIRST PLAYER TO CALL "SNAP!" WINS BOTH PILES...

Sooner or later, someone will turn up a card that matches a face-up card on another player's pile.

The first person to spot the pair (it might be 2 aces or 2 tens) and call out *"Snap!"* wins both piles. He adds them to the bottom of his heap, and play continues where it left off.

A player who calls wrongly forfeits the top card of his pile to the person whose card had just been turned over.

Players who run out of cards stay in the game until the next *"Snap!"* is called. If they don't win a pile then, they're out.

The winner is the player who finishes with all the cards.

Le Pouilleux

Number of Players: **3 to 7**

Number of Cards: **51**

Le Pouilleux (pronounced pooh-yeh) means *"The Lice-Man"* (ugh!) and is a French version of Old Maid but is played in a slightly different way.

Before you start, take out the jack of clubs and put it to one side; you won't need it. Deal

COLLECT PAIRS!

the rest of the cards face down among the players. Some people may get more cards than others but this doesn't matter.

Look at your hand carefully and take out any pairs of the same colour, say, the three of hearts and the three of diamonds, or the queen of spades and the queen of clubs, and place them in a pile on the table in front of you. When the other players have done the same, you're

PICK A CARD!

ready to start.

Get the player on your left to hold up her cards so that you can only see the backs. Then pick a card from her hand and add it to your own. If it makes a pair of the same colour with one you already hold, put those on your heap. If not, keep it.

Now it's the next player's turn to take an unknown card from the person on her left. And so on around the table. The idea is to make up as many pairs of the same colour as you can, and finish with no cards.

But remember, someone holds a jack of spades, Le Pouilleux, which can't be paired!

As soon as you run out of cards, drop out of the game. The others continue until just one player (the loser!) remains, stuck with the dreaded Lice-Man!

Old Maid

Number of Players: **3to7**

Number of Cards: **51**

Old Maid is better known than Le Pouilleux (except in France) and is much more widely played. The missing card in this game is the queen of spades. So remove it from the pack before you start.

The rules are identical to those for Le Pouilleux except that the pairs don't need to be the same colour. So, for example, you can pair off the three of diamonds with the three of clubs, or the ten of spades with the ten of hearts.

The loser is the player stuck with the card that can't be paired, one of the queens. She, of course is the *"Old Maid!"*

Go Fish

Number of Players: **3 to 5**

Number of Cards: **52**

Go Fish is another game in which players take cards from each other, so be on your toes.

To start, deal 5 cards face down to each person. The rest of the pack is left face down in the middle of the table.

Look closely at your hand. If you have 4 cards of the same worth, perhaps 4 kings or 4 threes, place them face up on the table in front of you. When the other players have done the same, you're ready to begin.

The object of the game is to collect as

SORT OUT SETS OF FOUR CARDS OF THE SAME KIND, AND PUT THEM ON THE TABLE IN FRONT OF YOU.

many of those sets of 4 as you can, either by taking cards from the stock or by *"robbing"* other players.

The person on the dealer's left goes first. She can ask any player to hand over every card of a particular worth that he holds (say, all his jacks or all his queens).

The only condition is that the person making the demand must hold at least one of those cards herself. If the player being asked has one of those cards named, too bad! He must hand them over!

WHEN YOU'RE TOLD
"GO FISH"
YOU MUST TAKE THE TOP CARD FROM THE PILE ON THE TABLE.

The *"robber"* adds them to her own cards, and gets another turn. As before she can ask any player to part with any cards (so long as she holds one herself). If she collects again, she can have yet another turn. And so on.

But the moment she picks a player who can't help, that player replies, *"Go fish!"* This means that the would-be robber must take the top card off the stock instead. And then it's the next player's turn to go.

But sometimes, by sheer chance, the card from the stock turns out to be exactly the one that was asked for. When this happens, the player must show the card (to prove it!) before putting it in her hand, and then she starts her turn all over again.

Any player who runs out of cards can take one from the top of the stock (when it's his turn) and then go on as before. When the stock is used up, players without cards are out of the game.

The winner is the person with the greatest number of sets when every card has been played.

Little Fish

Number of Players: **3 to 5**

Number of Cards: **52**

This is a simple form of Go Fish, so it's a great game to teach to younger children. You play it in the same way except that:

1. All the cards are dealt out (so there's no stock in the middle to worry about). It doesn't matter if some players get more cards than others.

2. You collect pairs (2 kings, 2 aces, etc.) instead of sets of 4.

The winner, of course, is the player with the most pairs when all the cards have been played.

This one is for Go Fish fans! It's played in much the same way as Go Fish, but with a diabolical difference!

In Authors, all the cards are dealt out first (just as they are in Little Fish). Then each player in turn tries to "rob" opponents.

But, and this is the catch, a player can only demand one card at a time. And he must name exactly which card he wants.

So if, for example, you're collecting jacks, you must name a particular one, say, the jack of diamonds, when you pounce on a victim.

And if your opponent has the jack of spades but not the jack of diamonds, she can turn you down. Tough!

The winner is the player with the most sets of 4 when all the cards are finally played. He'll also be the one with the sharpest eyes and longest memory.

Concentration

Number of Players: 3 to 7

Number of Cards: 52

Concentration is for people with good memories. Start by spreading all 52 cards face down on the table. The first player turns over any 2 cards so that everyone can see them. If he happens to turn over a pair (2 sevens, 2 kings, any 2 of the same value) he keeps them and has another go.

If not, the cards are replaced face down exactly where they came from, and it's the next player's chance to turn over any 2 cards and try to find a pair. Continue until all the cards are gone.

The winner is the player with the biggest pile of pairs at the end.

GO AGAIN
WHEN YOU
TURN UP
A PAIR!

57

Wot (some people call it Rockaway) is good fun for 2 players, and hilarious with 4 or more.

The dealer gives 7 cards to each player. The rest of the pack is left face down on the table, this is the "stock", except for the top card which is turned up and placed alongside the others.

The player on the dealer's left starts. The idea is to cover the turned-up card with another of the same suit or number. If you can't, you pick up a "forfeit", which is a card from the top of the stock, and let the next player have a turn.

The object of the game is to be the first player to hold no cards at all. If the stock runs out before someone wins, turn it and start a new pile going.

Aces and jokers are *"wild"*, which means you can play them when it's your turn no matter which card you were supposed to follow.

If you play a *"wild"* card, it's up to you to call a suit for the next player to follow, so you can choose one you know she doesn't hold!

Terrific! Losers collect 15 penalty marks for each ace or joker left in their hands, 10 for picture cards, and face numbers for others.

Quango is an advanced version of Wot, and much harder to win. The basic play is the same as for Wot. But there are 2 extra rules:

1. If you play a jack or an eight you have another turn.

2. If you play a seven, the next player must follow with another seven. If he doesn't have a seven, he must pick up 2 cards from the stock. If he can play a seven, then the following player faces the same problem and must either play a seven or pick up two cards. And so on around the table.

As in Wot, losers are stung with 15 penalty points for each ace or joker left in their hands at the finish, 10 for picture cards, and face numbers for the others. Good luck!

Cheat

Number of Players: **3 to 4**

Number of Cards: **52**

Here's a game for people who are good at telling lies! The better you are at making everyone believe that you're telling the truth when in fact you're not, the more chances you have of winning. So naturally, it's one of the most popular children's card games of all time.

It's best with 3 or 4 players, but you can have up to 6. If more than 4 play, you'll need 2 packs of cards shuffled together.

To start, deal all the cards 3 at a time face down among the players. Then give everyone a moment to sort through their hands.

The person on the dealer's left plays first. She must place 3 or 4 cards face down in the middle of the table.

They should be a matching set (say 3 jacks or 4 sixes). But since the cards are laid face down, nobody can tell.

"Three jacks!" she claims boldly.

True or false? If anyone doubts her word, now's the time to call out, *"Cheat!"*

When that happens, the game stops and the cards under suspicion are turned over. If they prove to be exactly as called, the accuser must pick up the pile and add all the cards in it to his own hand. If they prove to be phonies, the player who cheated collects them instead!

As I said, it's a game for good liars. If nobody accuses you of cheating, play passes to the next person. And so on around the table. You can claim to have laid down any 3 or 4 of a kind you like (there's no special order to follow) but if you fib and you're discovered, you pick up the whole pile, including the cards laid down before! If you're innocent, it's your accuser who suffers.

The winner is the person who gets rid of all his cards first.

Happy cheating!

Bon Débarras

Number of Players: **3to7**

Number of Cards: **52**

To play Bon Débarras (which is French for *"good riddance!"*) you need a fairly large table. And to play it well, you need to be good at dominoes.

Begin by dealing out all the cards face down among the players. The person on the left of the dealer starts by choosing any card from his hand and placing it face up in the middle of the table.

The next player to go must now place cards on both sides of and below the first card played. To the left, it must be a card of the same colour but exactly one spot lower in value. To the right, it must be the same colour but one spot higher. Below it must be the same number but a different colour.

Supposing the first card played is the seven of hearts, and the next player is lucky enough to be holding the six of diamonds, the eight of diamonds, and the seven of clubs. He can place the six to the left of the first card, the eight to the right, and the seven below. Great, three

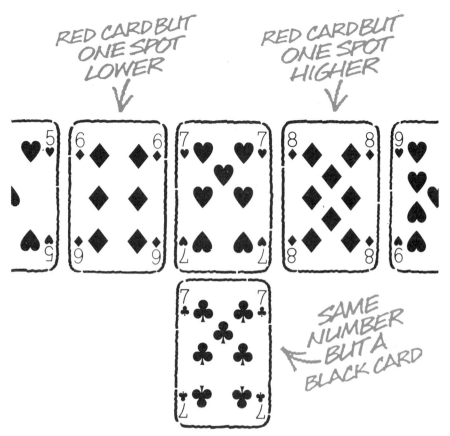

RED CARD BUT ONE SPOT LOWER

RED CARD BUT ONE SPOT HIGHER

SAME NUMBER BUT A BLACK CARD

cards unloaded in just one turn!

To follow, the next player needs a red five or a red nine to join the end of the line. Or a black six or eight to place alongside the card below.

If she can't go, she passes, and then it's up to the next person to add what he can. And so on until one of the players, the winner, gets rid of all his cards. The last cards in each line must be an ace at one end (next to a two) and a king at the other. And, of course, it helps a lot to get all 4 lines going as soon as possible.

Hearts

Number of Players: 4

Number of Cards: 52

Some people call this game *"Trumps"*. They shouldn't. For one thing that's not its name. For another, there aren't any trumps in it, and if you fall into the habit of thinking Hearts are trumps, you'll get into a mix-up when you play real trump games later on.

You need someone to keep score in Hearts, so find a pencil and paper before you begin.

Give the cards a good shuffle, and deal out the whole pack one by one, face down among the players. Everybody should have 13 cards.

The person on the dealer's left plays first by placing a card face up in the middle of the table. Then each player puts down a card in turn. Everyone must follow suit (which means they must play a card of the same suit as the first card played). Players without a card of that suit can put in any other card, but it will count below cards of the suit being followed.

The person who plays the best card (aces are highest) in the correct suit wins the trick, and he leads the first card of the next trick.

LOSE
5 POINTS

LOSE
4 POINTS

LOSE
3 POINTS

LOSE
2 POINTS

LOSE 1 POINT FOR
EACH SPOT CARD

THE PRICE YOU PAY FOR THE HEARTS YOU WIN!

The object of the game is to lose every trick containing a heart, particularly the jack, queen, king, and ace of hearts.

You collect one penalty point for every spot card heart you win, 2 penalty points for the jack, 3 for the queen, 4 for the king, and 5 for the ace.

On the other hand, if you pick up all the hearts (the whole 13!), (called *"shooting the moon"*) every penalty point is wiped out and you score zero.

The winner is the player with the least number of penalty points when the round ends.

Go Boom

Number of Players: 3 to 6

Number of Cards: 52

Go Boom is a game everybody seems to enjoy. Start by dealing 7 cards face down to each player. (You can deal 8 if there are just 3 of you, or 6 if there are 6 players).

Put the undealt part of the pack face down on the table.

The player on the dealer's left begins by placing any card he chooses from his hand face up into the middle of the table.

The next person must follow with a card of the same suit or same worth. So if the first player plays the jack of hearts, the next player must put down a heart or another jack. If she plays, say, the ten of hearts, the third player can play either a heart or a ten. And so on until every player has played either a heart or a card of the same worth as the one before.

The highest card played (aces are top) takes the trick, and the winner plays the first card of the next trick. When two or more cards of the same worth are played, the first played is highest.

YOU MUST PLAY A CARD OF THE SAME SUIT OR THE SAME WORTH AS THE ONE BEFORE...

...SO YOU'RE IN LUCK!

YOU CAN FOLLOW WITH EITHER THE JACK OF DIAMONDS (BECAUSE IT'S THE SAME SUIT) OR THE QUEEN OF HEARTS (BECAUSE IT'S ANOTHER QUEEN).

Players who can't follow suit (or match the previous card in worth) must keep taking cards from the top of the stock until they turn up one which can be played.

When the stock runs out, players who can't go miss a turn. The winner is the first player to get rid of all her cards.

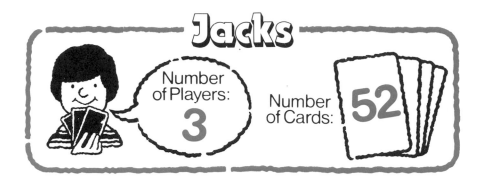

Jacks

Number of Players: **3**

Number of Cards: **52**

You may need a deck of small cards to play Jacks, also called Knaves, because there are a lot of cards to hold. But don't be put off, it's a terrific game.

Start by dealing the cards one at a time face down among the players. They should have 17 cards each. Place the last card face up in the middle of the table. That shows the trump suit.

The person on the dealer's left plays first by laying a card face up in the middle of the table. Then each player puts down a card in turn. Everyone must follow suit if possible (which means playing a card of the same suit as the one first played).

If you don't have a card of that kind, you're allowed to play a trump card. Trumps beat all other suits. If you don't play a trump, you can throw in any other card you choose, but it will count below cards of the suit being followed.

The person who plays the best card wins the trick, and plays the first card of the next trick.

MINUS 4. MINUS 3. MINUS 2. MINUS 1.

You score a point for every trick you win. But you lose points if any of them contain a jack.

Deduct 4 points for winning the jack of hearts, 3 points for the jack of diamonds, 2 for the jack of clubs, and 1 for the jack of spades.

The winner is the first player to get 20 points. And it's safest to choose the one who's best at adding to keep score.

KEV	TIM	SUE
+5	+4	+4
-0	-5	-5
+5	-1	-1

SCORE ONE POINT FOR
EVERY TRICK YOU WIN.
THEN TAKE AWAY POINTS
FOR CAPTURING JACKS!

Rolling Stone

Number of Players: **4 to 6**

Number of Cards: **32 to 48** DEPENDING ON NUMBER OF PLAYERS

This is a good one! It's best with 4 players, but you can have up to 6. With 4, you'll need 32 cards, so take out the sixes, fives, fours, threes, and twos before you begin. (If 5 play, keep the sixes and fives in; if 6 play add the fours and threes as well.)

To start, deal all the cards one at a time face down among the players. They should have 8 each.

The player on the dealer's left leads the first card. It can be any card of any suit. Let's say it's the ten of hearts.

The next player must then follow with another card of the same suit, perhaps the seven of hearts. The third player must also put down a heart. So must all the players.

Anyone who can't follow suit must pick up all the cards played so far and add them to his hand. Then he must play a new card to start a fresh round.

If everyone is able to follow, the player who

70

BAD LUCK!!

IF YOU CAN'T FOLLOW SUIT, YOU MUST PICK UP **ALL** THE CARDS PLAYED!

played the highest card collects the trick and makes it into a wastepile. Then he plays the first card (again, any that he chooses) of the next round. And so on until one player, the winner!, gets rid of all his cards.

In most games there will be several occasions when you can't follow suit, so you'll be stuck with the cards other players have played. Never mind, it's all part of the fun! And with everyone in the same boat, you could still end up the winner!

Blackjack

Number of Players: **3 to 10**

Number of Cards: **52**

Blackjack is one of the most popular card games ever invented. It's also known as *Twenty-one* or *Vingt-et-un*, and *Pontoon*, and there are versions played in casinos called *Baccarat* (the one James Bond is good at!).

The dealer is the most important person in Blackjack, so it's best to decide who it should be, and for how long, before you start.

Suppose it's you. Give the pack a good shuffle and deal out 2 cards face down to each player.

The idea is to collect cards with a higher

"STICK!"

"HIT ME!"

PICTURE CARDS COUNT AS 10.

ACES CAN BE EITHER 1 OR 11.

YOU BUST IF YOUR CARDS ADD UP TO MORE THAN 21!

score than anybody else.

The snag is that your score must not go above 21. If it does you *"bust"* and lose to everybody with an *"un-bust"* score, however low. Tricky!

Picture cards count as 10 each, aces are worth either one or 11, and spot cards go by face numbers. The dealer is against all the other players and must try to beat them. He asks each person in turn: "Will you stick or hit me?" A player who says *"stick!"* receives no more cards.

A player who says *"hit me!"* is dealt one further card. Then the dealer repeats his question, "stick or hit me?" If the player wants a fourth card, she says *"hit me!"* again, and so on until she has as many cards as she needs for a good score. Then she says *"stick!"* If she goes over 21, she must drop the cards face up on the table and declare: *"Bust!"*

When all the players have been served, the dealer turns over his own two cards and goes

THIS HAND = 19.

THIS HAND = 21.

BLACKJACK = 21.

"stick" or *"hit me"* for himself.

If the dealer goes over 21, he loses to everyone with 21 or less. If the dealer sticks at 21 or less, he loses to anyone whose total is closer to 21. When the dealer is closer to 21, he wins. A draw occurs whenever the dealer and a player have the same score.

You can play for chips or buttons if you like, but most children I know don't bother. They find it's exciting enough just playing for fun.

Coinchée

Number of Players: 4

Number of Cards: 32

Coinchée (pronounced *kwon-shay*) is a nail-biting French game for 4 people, 2 playing in partnership against the other 2.

It's the only partnership game you'll find in this book, and it had to be included because it's too good to leave out. So stand by for some exciting action. But be warned, you'll need eagle eyes and razor-sharp wits to play it well.

Like lots of French games, Coinchée is played with just 32 cards, so take out the twos, threes, fours, fives, and sixes before you begin.

Then decide on your partner, and arrange your chairs so that each person sits opposite his

TAKE OUT ALL THESE CARDS!

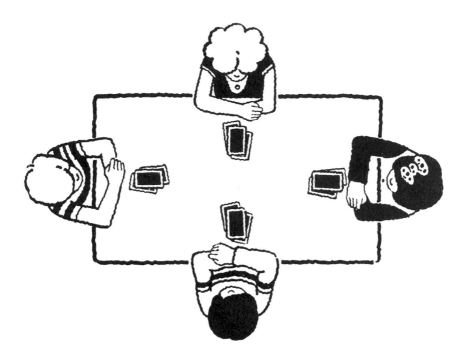

partner. To start, deal all the cards face down among the players. They should get 8 each. Try to deal the cards in batches: 3 to players first time around, 2 each next time, then 3 each again. When all the cards are dealt, the fun starts! The dealer's partner (sitting opposite)

DEAL IN BATCHES!

must leave his cards on the table and not look at them. The other players can pick up their hands to see what they have.

The dealer must then work out the best way she and her partner can beat the other two. To win, the two of them must capture *"tricks"* containing scoring cards. Tens count 5 points each, aces are worth 4, kings 3, queens 2, and jacks one. Everything else counts zero.

The partnership that picks up the most points wins the game. The dealer must decide:

1. Which suit will be trumps, or
2. There will be no trumps, or
3. Her partner should decide!

If she opts to take the plunge herself, she calls the name of the trump suit or explains, "No trumps this time!" But if she thinks her partner should choose, she says, "Over to you!" Now at last her partner can pick up his cards. If he has been given the job of naming trumps (or no trumps), he must do so. He can't pass the problem back to the dealer.

So, if you are dealing and you call "Over to you!", you're stuck with what your partner says.

After you (or your partner) have decided what to do, the opposition get their chance to speak up. If either of your opponents doubts that you can win the game, one of them may call, *"Coinchée!"*

SCORING CARDS

= 5 POINTS   = 4 POINTS   = 3 POINTS

= 2 POINTS   = 1 POINT   ALL OTHERS
                                    = 0

This is a challenge, and it doubles all the points scored!

If you still think you can beat them, you're entitled to respond, *"Sur coinchée!"* That multiplies the points score by 4. When all that's settled, the real game can begin.

The person on the dealer's left plays first. Then each player puts down a card in turn. Everyone must follow suit if possible (which means playing a card of the same suit as the first one played.)

And, if you have one, you must play a higher card of that suit than either of your opponents play. The order of seniority is:

ten (the top card), then the ace, king, queen, jack, nine, eight, and seven. If you don't have a card of the right suit, you're allowed to play a trump card. Trumps beat all other suits. If you don't play a trump, you can throw in any other card you choose, but it won't beat cards of the suit being followed.

The person who plays the best card wins the trick, and plays the first card of the next trick.

You get a point for every trick you win, as well as points for all scoring cards you collect.

At the end of the game, it's the next player's turn to deal. And so on around the table.

The winners are the pair who score the most points by the end of the session. And you had better agree on a time limit before you start.

F Good games for the family F

Rummy

Number of Players: 3 to 6

Number of Cards: 52

Rummy is one of the world's most popular card games. It has been played by so many people in so many countries for so many years that there are now dozens of different versions.

But once you've learned how to play basic Rummy, you'll find other Rummy games easy to understand.

DEAL 7 CARDS TO EACH PLAYER.

TURN OVER THE TOP CARD OF THE STOCK AND PLACE IT ALONGSIDE.

Start by dealing 7 cards face down to each player. (If there are more than 4 players, it's best to deal just 6).

Put the stock face down on the table. Then turn over the top card and place it face up alongside the others to start a wastepile.

The object of the game is to be the first player to get rid of all the cards in your hand. There are 3 ways to unload cards.

1. By collecting a set of 3 or more cards of the same worth, say 3 sevens or 4 queens, and laying them down on the table when it's your turn to play;

2. By collecting 3 or more cards of the same suit that run in sequence (like the two, three, and four of clubs, or the nine, ten, jack, and queen of diamonds) and laying them down when it's your turn;

3. By adding cards (again, when it's your turn to play) to a run or set already laid down.

The player on the dealer's left gets the first chance to put down his cards. If he can lay down all 7 at once, this is called a "rummy", the game is over!

If not, he must pick up either the top card on the wastepile or the (unknown) top card on the stock. One or the other will perhaps, help toward completing a set or run.

He can keep the card he takes (if it's useful)

and return any card in his hand to the wastepile. If the card from the stock is unhelpful, he can dump it straight on the wastepile.

When he has made his choice, it's the next player's turn. He must first pick up a card from the wastepile or the stock.

Then he may lay down a run or set, or add on to any cards played by the first player.

Third, he must throw out one of the cards in his hand and place it face up on the wastepile. At the end of his turn, it's the next player's turn to follow the same routine. And so on around the table.

You don't have to lay down any runs or sets, they can prove helpful to other players looking for places to off-load difficult cards. But you will be penalized for all cards remaining in your hand, including complete runs or sets, the moment another player puts down the last of his cards and is *"out"*. That's when the game ends.

MAKE **SEQUENCES** FROM THREE OR MORE CARDS OF THE SAME SUIT THAT RUN TOGETHER...

YOU LOSE POINTS FOR UNMATCHED CARDS...

You collect 10 penalty points for each picture card you hold, one penalty point for each ace, and the spot numbers on all others.

If the stock runs out before the game ends, the next player in turn can take either the top card of the wastepile or the first card of the new stock (which is formed by turning the wastepile over).

You can add to the cards laid down by all players at the table (including yourself) in different ways. If someone has laid down a set of, say, 3 queens, you can tag on the fourth queen if you have it.

You can add to a run, perhaps the four, five, and six of diamonds, at both ends: with the three at the bottom end, and the seven at the top. In fact, you can add as many cards as you like (top and bottom) to a laid-down run so long as the extra cards continue the proper sequence. And you can join several runs or sets at one time when it's your turn to play.

You'll need to keep your wits about you to spot all the possibilities, which is one of the reasons Rummy is such a fascinating game!

And, of course, you need a good scorer! It's best to agree how long you're going to play before you start.

The winner is the person with the lowest number of penalty points when time's up.

Round-the-Corner Rummy

Number of Players: 3 to 6

Number of Cards: 52

This is played like any other rummy game, with one important difference.

In Round-the-Corner Rummy, a sequence of cards can also go past the ace. This means you can lay down a king, an ace, and a two of the same suit to make up a sequence, which can be very useful.

THE ACE CAN FOLLOW THE KING IN YOUR SEQUENCE...

But watch out, aces count as 11 (instead of one) in the score!

This is a simpler version of basic Rummy, and you'll probably find it much more fun.

But you must know the basic Rummy rules first.

Queen City Rummy is played in the same way as basic Rummy, except that you must lay down all 7 cards in your hand at one time!

This means keeping hold of all your cards, even if they include complete runs or sets, until you're ready to lay down the whole hand.

The first player to do this (and call out *"Rummy!"*) is the winner. He collects 10 points for each picture card laid down, one point for each ace, and spot numbers on all others. Everybody else scores zero.

Wild Card Rummy

Number of Players: **3 to 6**

Number of Cards: **52**

This is the same as Queen City Rummy, but with the joker and twos *"wild."* This means they can be used as any cards you like. Great!

Score in the same way as for basic Rummy, but count 25 penalty points for each *"wild"* card left in your hand when the game ends.

Newmarket

Number of Players: **3 to 8**

Number of Cards: **56**

Newmarket is one of the oldest English card games, and there are many different versions of it around the world.

The one we've chosen (probably the most popular) is actually a combination of three different games. So perhaps it really shouldn't be called Newmarket at all!

Never mind, everybody knows it as

Newmarket so that's the title we're sticking with here.

It's played with a full pack of 52 cards plus 4 from another deck. The extra cards are an ace of spades, a king of hearts, queen of clubs, and jack of diamonds. Place these 4 face up in a square in the center of the table. They are the pay cards.

Before the game starts, each player must place a chip on one of the pay cards and put another chip in a pool or kitty. (If you don't have chips, you can use Monopoly money, beans, or buttons. Each player should be given the same number before the game begins.)

Start by choosing a dealer. The best way to do this is to let each player *"cut"* the pack. The player who cuts the highest card deals first. After that, it's taken in turn.

The dealer distributes all 52 cards, one at a time, face down among the players, but deals

YOU NEED THESE FOUR CARDS
FROM ANOTHER PACK...

2 hands for himself. Some players may get more cards than others but this doesn't matter.

The dealer looks at one of his hands. If he likes it, he keeps it. If not, he can swap it for his other hand. But, take care! He can't swap back if the second hand turns out to be worse than the first! The first hand is then put to one side, face down, and goes out of the game.

If the dealer decides not to swap, the spare hand is offered to the player on his left. If it's not wanted by her either, the offer passes to the next player. And so on around the table. If nobody wants to swap, the spare hand goes out of the game.

But that isn't likely! At least one of the players is sure to have been dealt a bad hand

LIFT OFF A BUNDLE OF CARDS
TO "CUT" THE PACK...

THE DEALER GETS **TWO** "HANDS" — AND A CHOICE!

and will be eager to exchange it! He must pay one chip into the pool as a *"swap fee"* (the dealer is the only player excused from paying) and must keep the new hand once she's looked at it.

When the business of the spare hand is sorted out, the game can start. The player on the dealer's left leads the first card. It can be any suit, but it must be the lowest card of the suit that she holds. She places it face up on the table in front of her and calls out the name.

Supposing it's the seven of clubs. The other players must now scan their hands to see which clubs they hold. Whoever has the next highest card in the sequence, the eight of clubs, must call "Eight!" and lay it down in front of him. Then the player with the nine of clubs does the same. And so on until somebody finally lays down the ace of clubs.

When the ace goes down, the person who played it must begin a new sequence. As before, she can play a card from any suit (even clubs again!), but it must be the lowest card of the suit in her hand.

Most sequences never reach the ace, they are blocked because the missing cards are in the spare hand, or because some higher cards have already been played. Whenever a sequence stops, the person who played last must begin again with the lowest card he has of the suit he wishes to play.

Sometimes the sequence will include a card that's the same as one of the pay cards in the middle of the table. Terrific! The player who plays it can pick up all the chips on that particular card.

There's also another prize to be won: the chips in the pool. They go to the first player to get rid of all his cards. When this happens, the game is over, and any chips still left on the pay cards must stay where they are to be played for in the next game.

Now you can see why it's important to

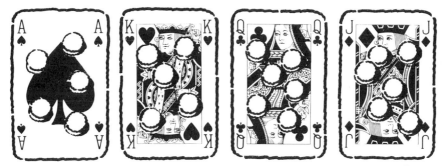

YOU PICK UP CHIPS ON THE CARDS
DURING PLAY...

...AND ALL THE
CHIPS IN THE POOL
IF YOU WIN THE GAME!

YOU CAN INTERRUPT
PLAY AT ANY TIME BY LAYING THE
NINE OF DIAMONDS—**SPINADO!**

collect on pay cards as quickly as possible. One special card in the pack can be your biggest ally, the nine of diamonds. It's a *"wild"* card and has been given a curious name: spinado.

If your hand includes spinado, you have an advantage over all the other players. For a start, it needn't be played in sequence. So when the eight of diamonds is played, you don't have to play the spinado next, and it's better not to!

Spinado is much more useful in another way, as a card you can play at any moment to interrupt the game. If you spot someone playing card after card and about to win the pool, play spinado quickly! It stops his run, and also gives you the chance to play the next card, so starting another sequence. Exciting stuff!

Michigan is played in exactly the same way as Newmarket but without *"spinado"*.

So the player holding the nine of diamonds does not have any special advantage. Shame...!

Double Stops

Number of Players: **3 to 8**

Number of Cards: **58**

Another game played like Newmarket, but with an extra prize to be won.

Before you start, add the nine and ten of hearts from the other deck to the pay cards layout. Make sure they overlap so that any chips put there are on both cards.

Crazy? No, it means you need to hold the 2 cards to collect!

If no one wins, the stakes stay there to be played for in the next game ... and the next ... and the next ...!